Florence Nightingale

Women of War - Book 7
History Nerds

Florence Nightingale
Women of War - Book 7
Copyright © 2024 History Nerds.
Written by History Nerds.

Table of Contents

Introduction

Throughout history, the narrative of war has often been dominated by tales of valor and heroism on the battlefield. However, an equally compelling and vital story exists in the contributions of women who have served in roles that, while not directly involving combat, have been crucial to the survival and well-being of soldiers and civilians alike. These women have fought their own battles, often in the shadows, providing care, solace, and essential services amidst the chaos of war. This introduction explores the significant impact of women in non-combat roles during times of conflict, with a particular focus on the legacy of Florence Nightingale, whose pioneering work laid the foundation for modern nursing and humanitarian efforts in war zones.

Florence Nightingale: A Beacon of Compassion and Reform

Florence Nightingale's name is synonymous with nursing and healthcare reform. Born into a wealthy British family in 1820, Nightingale defied societal expectations by pursuing a career in nursing, which at the time was considered an unsuitable profession for women of her status. Her determination and compassion led her to the battlefields of the Crimean War in 1854, where she and a team of nurses provided much-needed care to wounded soldiers.

Nightingale's work in the Scutari hospital revolutionized military healthcare. She implemented strict sanitary practices, significantly reducing the mortality rate. Her meticulous data collection and analysis demonstrated the importance of hygiene and proper medical care, influencing military and civilian healthcare systems worldwide. Nightingale's legacy extends beyond her immediate impact; she established nursing as a respected profession and set the stage for future generations of healthcare workers in conflict zones.

The Expanding Role of Women in War

Nightingale's pioneering efforts opened the door for countless women who followed in her footsteps, serving in various capacities during times of war. These women have worked as nurses, doctors, humanitarian aid workers, and support staff, each contributing to the war effort in invaluable ways.

The role of nurses during wartime cannot be overstated. From the Civil War to World Wars I and II, women have served as frontline medical personnel, often working in deplorable conditions to save lives. Clara Barton, known as the "Angel of the Battlefield" during the American Civil War, founded the American Red Cross, which has provided aid during countless conflicts. In World War I, nurses like Edith Cavell risked their lives to treat soldiers on both sides and were instrumental in saving the lives of countless combatants and civilians.

Beyond the immediate battlefield, women have also been pivotal in providing humanitarian aid. Organizations such as the International Committee of the Red Cross

(ICRC) and Médecins Sans Frontières (Doctors Without Borders) have relied on the dedication and bravery of female aid workers to deliver food, medical supplies, and other essential services in war-torn regions. These women often work under extreme danger, facing the same threats as soldiers but without the protection of weapons or military force.

The psychological toll of war is immense, and women have played critical roles in providing mental health support to soldiers and civilians affected by conflict. During World War II, for instance, the American Red Cross' "Donut Dollies" not only served refreshments but also offered a comforting presence to troops, boosting morale and providing a semblance of normalcy amidst the horrors of war. Today, female psychologists and counselors continue this work, addressing the mental health needs of those impacted by conflict.

In contemporary conflicts, the role of women in non-combat capacities has expanded even further. Women now serve in various roles within military and non-governmental organizations, contributing to peacekeeping, reconstruction, and development efforts in war-torn regions.

Women have increasingly taken on roles as peacekeepers and mediators in conflict zones. The United Nations has recognized the importance of including women in peacekeeping missions, understanding that they bring unique perspectives and skills that are essential for successful conflict resolution and post-war reconstruction. Women peacekeepers often engage with local communities, advocating for women's rights and helping to rebuild trust and social cohesion.

Many women have become vocal advocates and activists, fighting for the rights of those affected by war. Malala Yousafzai, though primarily known for her advocacy for girls' education, has also spoken out about the impacts of war on children and education. Her efforts highlight the broader consequences of conflict and the need for comprehensive support systems for affected populations.

Women continue to lead in medical innovation and leadership within war zones. Dr. Hawa Abdi, a Somali doctor, and human rights activist, established a hospital, school, and refuge for displaced people in Somalia, providing critical services in one of the most dangerous regions in the world. Her work exemplifies the extraordinary contributions of women in non-combat roles, offering hope and healing in the darkest of times.

The contributions of women in non-combat roles during times of war are indispensable. From Florence Nightingale's groundbreaking work in military healthcare to the tireless efforts of contemporary female humanitarian workers, these women have shown exceptional courage, resilience, and dedication. They have not only saved lives and alleviated suffering but have also paved the way for future generations of women to serve in critical capacities during times of conflict. As we honor their legacy, it is essential to recognize and support the ongoing efforts of women who continue to serve on the frontlines of humanitarian aid, medical care, and peacebuilding in war zones around the world. Their work is a testament to the profound impact that compassion and dedication can have, even amidst the devastation of war.

Chapter 1: From Obscurity to Legend

A Timeline of Transformation

Florence Nightingale's life transformed from a privileged upbringing to becoming the founder of modern nursing. Her journey was a remarkable series of defining moments that shaped her destiny and revolutionized global healthcare. This timeline chronicles the key milestones, revealing how her dedication, intellect, and pioneering spirit led to groundbreaking reforms still influencing nursing today.

Florence Nightingale was born into an affluent and influential British family on May 12, 1820, in Florence, Italy, hence her namesake. Her parents, William Edward Nightingale and Frances Nightingale, belonged to the upper echelons of society, providing her with a life of luxury and privilege. The Nightingales were well-educated and culturally refined, and they ensured that their daughters, Florence and her older sister Parthenope, received an excellent education, which was uncommon for women at that time.

Florence's childhood was characterized by a comfortable and cultured environment, marked by frequent travels across Europe and exposure to intellectual discourse. Despite this privileged upbringing, Florence was not content with a life of leisure and social obligations. From a young age, she exhibited a keen intellect and a sense of purpose that extended beyond the confines of her societal status. She was deeply interested in the welfare of others, often visiting the sick and the poor in her community, a trait that set her apart from her peers.

Her parents, particularly her mother, expected Florence to marry well and fulfill her role as a society lady. However, Florence harbored a profound sense of destiny that called her to a greater purpose. She was acutely aware of the suffering and illness that afflicted many, and she felt compelled to make a difference. This inner calling would eventually lead her to defy societal norms and pursue a career in nursing, a profession that was not only undervalued but also deemed inappropriate for women of her social standing.

In 1837, at the age of 17, Florence Nightingale had a life-changing experience that would shape her future. She described it as a divine calling, a moment of profound epiphany in which she felt summoned by God to serve others through nursing. This spiritual awakening ignited an unwavering commitment to improving healthcare and the well-being of the sick and vulnerable. Nightingale's vision extended beyond individual care to encompass systemic changes in healthcare practices and policies.

This calling was not just a fleeting sentiment; it was a powerful and enduring force that guided her actions and decisions. Nightingale began to see nursing as her vocation, a means through which she could fulfill her spiritual and moral duty. She believed that this divine mandate required her to dedicate her life to the service of others, despite the societal expectations and obstacles she would face.

Nightingale's commitment was further strengthened by her observations of the inadequate and often appalling conditions in hospitals and other healthcare settings of the time. She recognized that many illnesses and deaths were preventable and that proper care, sanitation, and management could save lives. This realization fueled her determination to acquire the knowledge and skills necessary to reform nursing and healthcare.

Despite her family's initial disapproval and the prevailing societal norms, Nightingale's sense of purpose remained unshaken. She embarked on a journey of self-education, studying the practices of nursing and healthcare across Europe. This period of learning and observation would later inform her revolutionary ideas and practices in nursing.

In 1844, Florence Nightingale made a bold decision to pursue nursing, a profession that was widely regarded as unsuitable for women of her social class. At that time, nursing was often associated with low-status work, typically performed by untrained women or those from lower socio-economic backgrounds. It was certainly not a profession considered appropriate for someone of Nightingale's privileged upbringing.

Her decision to become a nurse was met with significant resistance from her family. Her parents, particularly her mother, were horrified at the thought of their daughter engaging in what they considered menial and degrading work. They had envisioned a different future for Florence, one that involved marriage and a life of social engagements rather than tending to the sick and the poor.

Despite this opposition, Nightingale was resolute in her decision. She was driven by her sense of divine calling and her passion for making a meaningful impact on the lives of others. Recognizing the need for proper training and education, she embarked on a rigorous program of self-education. She studied the practices and theories of healthcare and nursing, drawing on the works of leading medical practitioners and visiting hospitals across Europe to observe their methods.

Nightingale's travels took her to places like Kaiserswerth in Germany, where she trained under Pastor Theodor Fliedner and the deaconesses. This experience was instrumental in shaping her understanding of nursing and hospital management. She also visited hospitals in Paris and other European cities, absorbing a wealth of knowledge about hygiene, patient care, and medical practices.

Her self-directed education was comprehensive and thorough, equipping her with the knowledge and skills that would later revolutionize nursing. Nightingale's determination to learn and her willingness to defy societal norms set her apart as a pioneer in the field. Her relentless pursuit of excellence and her commitment to her calling laid the foundation for her future achievements in nursing and healthcare reform.

In 1853, Florence Nightingale's nursing vocation was realized when she was appointed superintendent of the Institute for the Care of Sick Gentlewomen in Distressed Circumstances in London. This role provided her with a platform to apply the extensive knowledge and skills she had acquired through years of self-education and observation. It was a pivotal moment in her career, marking the transition from theory to practice.

As superintendent, Nightingale was responsible for overseeing the care of sick and impoverished gentlewomen, many of whom had fallen on hard times. The institute was one of the few places that offered care to women of higher social standing who were in financial distress, providing a unique challenge and opportunity for Nightingale. Her role involved managing the day-to-day operations of the facility, ensuring that patients received proper care, and implementing improvements to the institution's practices.

Nightingale approached her duties with the same dedication and meticulous attention to detail that had characterized her studies. She introduced systematic record-keeping and data analysis to monitor patient outcomes and identify areas for improvement. Her emphasis on hygiene, nutrition, and proper sanitation began to show tangible results, as the health and recovery rates of patients improved under her supervision.

This position also allowed Nightingale to put into practice her ideas about nursing as a profession. She emphasized the importance of training and education for nurses, advocating for a more structured and professional approach to nursing care. Her leadership and organizational skills were evident as she worked to improve the standards of care at the institute.

Nightingale's success at the Institute for the Care of Sick Gentlewomen demonstrated her capability and commitment to nursing. It also solidified her reputation as a competent and innovative healthcare professional. This role was instrumental in preparing her for the challenges she would face during the Crimean War, where her efforts would gain international recognition and forever change the landscape of nursing and healthcare.

In 1854, as the Crimean War raged, Florence Nightingale embarked on one of the most challenging and defining missions of her career. Responding to reports of appalling conditions and high mortality rates among wounded soldiers, she led a team of 38 volunteer nurses to the Barrack Hospital in Scutari, Turkey. This decision marked a turning point in her life and in the history of nursing.

Upon arrival, Nightingale and her team were confronted with horrific conditions that were far worse than they had anticipated. The hospital was severely overcrowded, with injured soldiers lying in filthy, cramped wards. The lack of basic sanitation and hygiene was shocking, with vermin and disease rampant throughout the facility. Supplies were scarce, and medical equipment was often inadequate or nonexistent. The stench of illness and decay permeated the air, and the mortality rate among patients was alarmingly high.

Nightingale immediately recognized that drastic measures were needed to address the dire situation. She set to work with her characteristic determination and organizational acumen. She and her team began by thoroughly cleaning the wards, implementing rigorous hygiene practices, and improving ventilation. They also established systems for better nutrition, ensuring that patients received adequate and nutritious food to aid in their recovery.

The conditions in Scutari were not only physically challenging but also emotionally taxing. Nightingale's compassion and dedication were evident as she tirelessly tended to the soldiers, often working late into the night. Her nightly rounds through the wards, carrying a lamp to check on the patients, earned her the enduring nickname "The Lady with the Lamp." This image of Nightingale became iconic, symbolizing her unwavering commitment and care.

Nightingale's efforts in Scutari had a profound impact. Under her leadership, the hospital's mortality rate dropped dramatically from 42% to 2%. Her implementation of sanitary practices and improved care standards saved countless lives and set a new precedent for military and civilian hospitals alike. Her work in the Crimean War brought her international acclaim and cemented her reputation as a pioneering nurse and healthcare reformer.

The experience at the Barrack Hospital in Scutari was a testament to Nightingale's resilience, ingenuity, and compassion. It showcased her ability to transform healthcare environments and underscored the importance of proper nursing care, hygiene, and organizational efficiency. Nightingale's legacy from the Crimean War would continue to influence healthcare practices long after the war had ended.

Between 1854 and 1856, Florence Nightingale's transformative work at the Barrack Hospital in Scutari became a seminal moment in the history of nursing and healthcare. Her rigorous enforcement of hygiene, improved ventilation, and the provision of nutritious food had a profound impact on the hospital environment and patient outcomes. This period of intense and dedicated effort showcased her exceptional leadership and set new standards for medical care.

One of Nightingale's first priorities was to address the appalling sanitary conditions that were contributing to the high mortality rates. She instituted a comprehensive cleaning regimen, ensuring that the wards were scrubbed and disinfected regularly. This emphasis on cleanliness was revolutionary at a time when the link between hygiene and health was not widely understood. Her efforts to improve sanitation dramatically reduced the spread of infections and disease within the hospital.

Nightingale also recognized the importance of proper ventilation in preventing illness. She implemented measures to improve airflow within the wards, reducing the concentration of pathogens and creating a healthier environment for patients. This focus on ventilation was a forward-thinking approach that contributed significantly to the reduction in mortality rates.

Nutrition was another critical area of reform. Nightingale ensured that patients received adequate and nutritious meals, understanding that proper diet was essential for recovery.

She organized the preparation and distribution of food, ensuring that it met the dietary needs of the wounded soldiers. This attention to nutrition not only improved patient outcomes but also set a precedent for the importance of dietary care in hospitals.

Nightingale's nightly rounds through the wards, carrying a lamp, became a powerful symbol of her dedication and compassion. These rounds were more than just routine checks; they were moments of personal connection and care. Her presence provided comfort and reassurance to the soldiers, many of whom were far from home and in great distress. This practice earned her the affectionate moniker "The Lady with the Lamp," a title that reflected her nurturing spirit and unwavering commitment to her patients.

The impact of Nightingale's work in Scutari was evident in the dramatic reduction of the hospital's mortality rate. This remarkable achievement highlighted the effectiveness of her methods and underscored the importance of proper nursing care, sanitation, and organizational efficiency. Her success in transforming the Barrack Hospital had far-reaching implications, influencing healthcare practices in military and civilian hospitals around the world.

Nightingale's work during the Crimean War not only saved countless lives but also elevated the status of nursing as a profession. Her methods and principles became foundational elements of modern nursing practice, emphasizing the importance of evidence-based care, hygiene, patient observation, and compassionate service. The legacy of "The Lady with the Lamp" continues to inspire and guide nurses and healthcare professionals to this day.

In 1856, Florence Nightingale returned to England as a national hero. Her groundbreaking work during the Crimean War had brought her widespread acclaim and recognition. The British public and government hailed her as a savior of soldiers and a pioneer in healthcare reform. However, Nightingale's mission was far from complete. Her experiences in the Crimean War fueled her determination to advocate for sanitary reforms in both military and civilian hospitals.

Upon her return, Nightingale was greeted with an outpouring of admiration and gratitude. The press, the public, and even Queen Victoria lauded her contributions. She was awarded numerous honors and financial rewards, which she chose to use to further her work in healthcare reform. Despite her newfound celebrity status, Nightingale remained focused on her goal of improving medical care and sanitation.

Nightingale's firsthand experiences in Scutari had exposed her to the dire consequences of inadequate sanitation and poor hospital management. She was acutely aware that the conditions she had encountered in the Crimean War were not unique to military hospitals but were prevalent in civilian healthcare facilities as well. This realization drove her to campaign tirelessly for systemic changes.

One of her first major initiatives was the establishment of the Nightingale Fund, which she used to promote the education and training of nurses. With the funds she had received, Nightingale founded the Nightingale Training School for Nurses at St. Thomas' Hospital in London in 1860. This institution became a model for nursing education worldwide, emphasizing rigorous training, practical skills, and professional standards.

Nightingale also delved into research and statistical analysis to support her advocacy for sanitary reforms. She meticulously documented the conditions and outcomes in hospitals, using her findings to build a compelling case for change. Her work in statistics was pioneering; she was one of the first to use visual data representations, such as pie charts, to illustrate the impact of sanitation on health outcomes.

Her efforts extended to advising government bodies and military authorities on healthcare policies. Nightingale worked closely with the Royal Commission on the Health of the Army, established in 1857, to investigate and address the health and sanitation issues in the British military. Her recommendations led to significant improvements in the design, organization, and management of military hospitals, as well as in the training and deployment of medical personnel.

Nightingale's influence reached beyond the military. She was a vocal advocate for public health reforms, emphasizing the need for clean water, proper sewage disposal, and adequate ventilation in hospitals and urban areas. Her work laid the foundation for modern public health policies and practices, contributing to a significant reduction in mortality rates and the improvement of overall health standards.

Florence Nightingale's return to England marked the beginning of a new phase in her career, one that was characterized by relentless advocacy and reform. Her experiences in the Crimean War had given her the knowledge, authority, and determination to drive significant changes in healthcare, benefiting countless individuals and shaping the future of nursing and public health.

In 1859, Florence Nightingale published her seminal work, "Notes on Nursing: What It Is and What It Is Not," which laid the foundation for modern nursing practices. This influential book was not just a manual for nurses but a comprehensive guide to healthcare, emphasizing the importance of evidence-based practices, patient observation, environment, and prevention. "Notes on Nursing" became a bestseller and was translated into multiple languages, reaching a global audience and significantly impacting the field of nursing.

"Notes on Nursing" was groundbreaking in its approach, offering practical advice and principles that were rooted in Nightingale's extensive experience and meticulous observations. The book addressed a wide range of topics, from hygiene and nutrition to the management of patient care and the importance of a healing environment. Nightingale's emphasis on sanitation, proper ventilation, and clean water was revolutionary at a time when the connection between hygiene and health was not fully understood.

One of the key themes of "Notes on Nursing" was the importance of patient observation. Nightingale stressed that careful and continuous observation was crucial for understanding a patient's condition and for providing effective care. She argued that nurses should be trained to observe patients' symptoms, behaviors, and responses to treatment, using this information to make informed decisions about their care. This focus on observation laid the groundwork for the development of clinical skills and diagnostic practices in nursing.

Nightingale also highlighted the significance of the environment in patient care. She believed that a clean, well-ventilated, and quiet environment was essential for healing and recovery. Her book provided detailed recommendations for hospital design, ward layout, and the maintenance of sanitary conditions. She advocated for the separation of patients with contagious diseases, the use of fresh air and natural light, and the importance of maintaining a calm and orderly atmosphere.

Prevention was another central aspect of Nightingale's philosophy. She argued that many illnesses and complications could be prevented through proper hygiene, nutrition, and preventive care. Her book emphasized the role of nurses in educating patients and their families about healthy practices and the importance of maintaining a clean and healthy living environment. This focus on prevention was ahead of its time and contributed to the development of public health nursing.

"Notes on Nursing" was more than just a textbook; it was a call to action for the professionalization of nursing. Nightingale's writing underscored the need for formal training and education for nurses, advocating for the establishment of nursing schools and the standardization of nursing practices. Her book became a cornerstone of nursing education, influencing curricula and shaping the development of the nursing profession worldwide.

The publication of "Notes on Nursing" marked a significant milestone in

Nightingale's career and in the history of healthcare. It established her as a leading authority on nursing and healthcare reform and provided a comprehensive framework for modern nursing practice. The principles and practices outlined in the book continue to be relevant and influential, reflecting Nightingale's enduring legacy as a pioneer of evidence-based care and patient-centered nursing.

In 1860, Florence Nightingale took a monumental step towards professionalizing nursing by founding the Nightingale Training School for Nurses at St. Thomas' Hospital in London. This pioneering institution was established with the aim of providing rigorous and comprehensive training for nurses, combining theoretical education with practical skills. The creation of the Nightingale Training School set a global standard for nursing education and played a crucial role in elevating the status of nursing as a respected and essential profession.

Nightingale's vision for the school was rooted in her belief that nursing required a high level of skill, knowledge, and dedication. She recognized that the quality of patient care depended largely on the competence and professionalism of nurses. To achieve this, she developed a curriculum that emphasized both theoretical learning and hands-on practice, ensuring that students were well-prepared to meet the demands of nursing.

The theoretical component of the curriculum covered a wide range of subjects, including anatomy, physiology, hygiene, and medical procedures. Nightingale believed that a strong foundation in these areas was essential for nurses to understand the complexities of patient care and to make informed decisions. She also included lessons on the principles of sanitation, nutrition, and patient observation, reflecting her holistic approach to healthcare.

Practical training was a cornerstone of the Nightingale Training School. Students were given extensive clinical experience, working alongside experienced nurses and physicians in the hospital wards. This hands-on training allowed them to apply their theoretical knowledge in real-world settings, honing their skills and gaining confidence in their abilities. Nightingale's emphasis on practical experience ensured that graduates of the school were not only knowledgeable but also capable and competent caregivers.

The establishment of the Nightingale Training School had a profound impact on the nursing profession. It set a new standard for nursing education, emphasizing the importance of formal training and professional development. The school's graduates, known as Nightingale Nurses, became highly sought after for their expertise and dedication. Many of them went on to establish nursing schools and training programs in other parts of the world, spreading Nightingale's principles and practices globally.

Nightingale's influence extended beyond the training of nurses. She was also deeply involved in the management and organization of the school, ensuring that it operated efficiently and effectively. Her meticulous attention to detail and commitment to excellence were reflected in every aspect of the institution, from the curriculum to the administration.

The success of the Nightingale Training School was a testament to Nightingale's vision and determination. It demonstrated that nursing was a profession that required specialized education and training, and it helped to raise the standards of healthcare across the board. The school's model of combining theory with practice became a blueprint for nursing education worldwide, shaping the development of the profession for generations to come.

Florence Nightingale's founding of the Nightingale Training School was a transformative moment in the history of nursing. It professionalized the field, established rigorous standards for education and practice, and ensured that nurses were equipped with the knowledge and skills necessary to provide high-quality care. The legacy of the Nightingale Training School continues to influence nursing education and practice, reflecting Nightingale's enduring impact on the healthcare profession.

Between 1883 and 1893, Florence Nightingale's influence extended beyond nursing to encompass broad public health advocacy. Her work during this period focused on improving sanitation, housing conditions for the poor, and the establishment of district nursing services. Nightingale's meticulous statistical analyses of mortality rates and health outcomes played a crucial role in driving policy improvements and advancing public health initiatives.

One of Nightingale's significant contributions to public health was her advocacy for improved sanitation. Drawing on her experiences during the Crimean War and her extensive research, she understood the critical link between hygiene and health. Nightingale campaigned vigorously for better sanitary practices, including the provision of clean water, proper sewage disposal, and improved waste management. Her efforts were instrumental in the development and implementation of public health policies that significantly reduced the incidence of infectious diseases.

Nightingale's concern for the living conditions of the poor also led her to advocate for better housing. She recognized that overcrowded and unsanitary living environments were major contributors to poor health and high mortality rates. Through her writings and public speaking, Nightingale highlighted the need for housing reforms, calling for the construction of well-ventilated and hygienic dwellings. Her work helped to raise awareness about the importance of healthy living conditions and influenced housing policies aimed at improving the quality of life for the urban poor.

Another important aspect of Nightingale's public health advocacy was her support for district nursing. She believed that healthcare should be accessible to all, regardless of their socio-economic status. To this end, she promoted the establishment of district nursing services, where trained nurses would provide medical care and health education in the homes of the poor and sick. This model of community-based nursing helped to extend healthcare services to underserved populations and laid the groundwork for modern public health nursing.

Nightingale's use of statistical analysis was pioneering and played a key role in her advocacy efforts. She was one of the first to employ rigorous data collection and analysis to identify health trends and outcomes. Her statistical work provided compelling evidence for the effectiveness of sanitary reforms and other public health measures. Nightingale's innovative use of visual data representations, such as her famous "coxcomb" charts, helped to communicate complex statistical information in a clear and persuasive manner.

Her analyses revealed stark disparities in mortality rates between different populations and highlighted the impact of social determinants of health. These findings were critical in advocating for policy changes and resource allocation to address health inequalities. Nightingale's ability to present data in an accessible and impactful way helped to convince policymakers and the public of the need for comprehensive public health reforms.

During this period, Nightingale's influence reached its zenith. She corresponded with and advised prominent political and medical figures, shaping public health policies and practices. Her work laid the foundation for many of the public health advances that followed, including the establishment of health departments, the implementation of sanitation laws, and the development of modern epidemiology.

Florence Nightingale's contributions between 1883 and 1893 were instrumental in advancing public health. Her advocacy for sanitation, better housing, and district nursing services, combined with her pioneering use of statistical analysis, drove significant policy improvements and helped to shape the future of public health. Her legacy as a visionary reformer and advocate for the well-being of all continues to inspire and guide public health efforts today.

In 1907, Florence Nightingale achieved a historic milestone by becoming the first woman to be awarded the Order of Merit by King Edward VII. This prestigious honor was a testament to her extraordinary contributions to nursing, healthcare, and public health. The award recognized Nightingale's visionary status and her enduring impact on the medical field and society at large.

The Order of Merit was established in 1902 by King Edward VII as a special distinction for individuals who had rendered exceptionally meritorious service in the fields of the arts, learning, literature, and science. Being the first woman to receive this honor was a significant acknowledgment of Nightingale's groundbreaking work and her role as a trailblazer in the advancement of nursing and healthcare.

By 1907, Nightingale's achievements were widely celebrated and her influence was well-established. Her pioneering efforts during the Crimean War, her establishment of the Nightingale Training School for Nurses, and her extensive contributions to public health had already cemented her reputation as a leading figure in healthcare reform. The awarding of the Order of Merit further solidified her legacy as a visionary and a transformative leader.

The honor was also a recognition of Nightingale's relentless dedication and tireless advocacy. Despite facing numerous challenges and societal barriers, she had persevered in her mission to improve healthcare and uplift the nursing profession. The Order of Merit symbolized the high regard in which she was held by her contemporaries and the lasting impact of her work on future generations.

Nightingale's receipt of the Order of Merit was not just a personal accolade; it was a milestone for women in the fields of medicine and public health. It highlighted the significant contributions that women could make to society and helped to pave the way for greater recognition and opportunities for women in healthcare and other professional fields. Her achievement inspired countless women to pursue careers in nursing and medicine, breaking down barriers and challenging stereotypes.

The award also underscored Nightingale's role as a pioneer in the use of statistical analysis and evidence-based practices. Her meticulous data collection and analysis had revolutionized the understanding of healthcare outcomes and had driven significant improvements in hospital management, sanitation, and public health policies. The Order of Merit recognized the scientific and methodological rigor that she brought to her work, which was instrumental in transforming nursing into a respected and professional discipline.

Receiving the Order of Merit was a fitting tribute to Nightingale's lifelong dedication to the service of others. It acknowledged her profound impact on healthcare and her visionary leadership in advancing the principles of compassionate, evidence-based care. Nightingale's legacy as the "Lady with the Lamp" was further cemented by this honor, which celebrated her contributions to humanity and her role as a beacon of hope and progress in the field of healthcare.

Florence Nightingale's receipt of the Order of Merit in 1907 remains a significant historical event, highlighting her exceptional achievements and her lasting influence on nursing and public health. It serves as a reminder of her pioneering spirit, her commitment to improving the lives of others, and her enduring legacy as a visionary reformer and advocate for healthcare excellence.

On August 13, 1910, Florence Nightingale passed away at the age of 90, leaving behind an enduring legacy that forever transformed the field of nursing and healthcare. Her life was marked by extraordinary compassion, unwavering dedication, and a pioneering commitment to evidence-based care. Nightingale's contributions laid the foundation for modern nursing practice and continue to inspire healthcare professionals around the world.

Nightingale's impact on nursing was profound and multifaceted. She is best remembered for her work during the Crimean War, where her efforts to improve sanitary conditions and provide compassionate care dramatically reduced mortality rates among wounded soldiers. Her iconic image as "The Lady with the Lamp," tending to patients during her nightly rounds, became a symbol of selfless service and dedication.

Beyond her wartime achievements, Nightingale's influence extended to the professionalization of nursing. She recognized the need for formal education and training for nurses, founding the Nightingale Training School for Nurses at St. Thomas' Hospital in London in 1860. This institution set the global standard for

 nursing education, emphasizing rigorous training, practical skills, and professional standards. The principles she established at the school became the cornerstone of modern nursing practice.

Nightingale was also a pioneering advocate for public health and sanitation. Her meticulous research and statistical analysis provided compelling evidence for the importance of hygiene, ventilation, and proper nutrition in preventing disease and improving health outcomes. She used her findings to advocate for systemic reforms in both military and civilian healthcare, influencing public health policies and practices worldwide.

Throughout her life, Nightingale remained committed to advancing the nursing profession and improving healthcare for all. Her work was characterized by a holistic approach to patient care, emphasizing the importance of the environment, nutrition, and psychological well-being. She believed that nursing was not just a profession but a calling, requiring compassion, empathy, and a deep commitment to the well-being of others.

Nightingale's legacy is also evident in her contributions to nursing theory and research. Her writings, including the seminal "Notes on Nursing," provided a comprehensive framework for nursing practice and education. Her emphasis on evidence-based care, patient observation, and preventive measures has had a lasting impact on the field, shaping the development of nursing as a scientific and professional discipline.

Florence Nightingale's death in 1910 marked the end of an era, but her influence continues to resonate. She left behind a legacy of compassion, dedication, and innovation that has inspired generations of nurses and healthcare professionals. Her life and work serve as a reminder of the profound difference that one individual can make in the world, driven by a commitment to improving the lives of others.

In recognition of her contributions, Nightingale has been honored in numerous ways, including the establishment of the International Nurses Day on her birthday, May 12. Her legacy is celebrated in nursing schools, hospitals, and healthcare institutions around the globe, where her principles of care, compassion, and evidence-based practice remain at the heart of nursing.

Florence Nightingale's enduring legacy is a testament to her visionary leadership and her unwavering commitment to the advancement of healthcare. Her life's work has left an indelible mark on the nursing profession, and her principles continue to guide and inspire those who follow in her footsteps..

Nightingale Vs. The Status Quo

Being born into a wealthy British family in 1820 nursing was considered unfit for ladies of Florence's status. Despite societal expectations, she felt a calling to care for the sick and suffering. In 1854, she defied convention and volunteered to lead nurses to the Crimean War after reports of appalling military hospital conditions shocked the British public.

Upon arriving at the Scutari Barracks Hospital in Constantinople (now Istanbul), Nightingale confronted utter despair. The overcrowded hospital had wounded soldiers lying on filthy floors with soaked, bloody bandages. Disease stench filled the air as rats scurried among patients - far from the clean, orderly hospitals she envisioned.

Nightingale's challenge was immense. Not only did she face horrific conditions, but military doctors resisted her presence as an unwelcome intrusion. Undaunted, she implemented radical reforms revolutionizing patient care.

Her first priority was sanitation. Recognizing filthy conditions bred disease and infection, she insisted on rigorous cleaning, changed linens regularly, opened windows for fresh air, and established a laundry service. Next, she turned to nutrition, working to prepare fresh, nutritious meals and special diets for the sickest patients.

Perhaps her most significant contribution emphasized compassionate care. She recognized healing required tending to emotional and spiritual needs too. Nightingale and her nurses spent countless hours listening to soldiers' stories, writing letters home, and offering comfort.

Nightingale introduced revolutionary round-the-clock nursing shifts ensuring patients were never unattended. She kept meticulous records, using statistics to identify patterns and advocate for reforms.

Back home, Nightingale's "Lady with the Lamp" image tending the sick became iconic.

Her advocacy led to reforms through the Royal Commission on Army Health. But her legacy extends far beyond Crimea - she envisioned professional nursing rooted in science, hygiene, and compassion.

Upon returning to England, she established the Nightingale Training School, the world's first secular nursing school. Its curriculum emphasized practical skills but also character, discipline, and empathy essential for good nurses. Her "Nightingale Nurses" established practices worldwide, spreading her vision.

Nightingale transformed nursing into a respected, essential profession. She pioneered handwashing, sanitation cornerstones, and championed dignity and compassionate care for all patients regardless of status. Today, she continues inspiring nurses worldwide to uphold compassion, dedication, and the highest care standards.

Her Crimean lessons on cleanliness, nutrition, and compassion remain vital in our era of advanced medicine when we can lose sight of basics. Her data-driven approach seems remarkably modern with electronic records and healthcare analytics. Most importantly, her story powerfully reminds us of one dedicated individual's impact against all odds.

As we reflect on Florence Nightingale's journey from Crimea to St. Thomas' Hospital, her example challenges us to strive for the highest care, compassion, and commitment standards. Her legacy calls us to uphold the belief that every life is precious, even amidst 21st century healthcare challenges.

Florence Nightingale's approach to healthcare contrasted sharply with the norms of her time. It was as striking as the light and darkness that earned her the name "The Lady with the Lamp." In that era, sanitation was largely ignored. Medical practices often followed tradition rather than science. The very idea of nursing as a profession barely existed. Nightingale's methods were revolutionary.

To understand her significance, one must grasp healthcare's dire state in the mid-19th century. Military hospitals were overcrowded, unsanitary breeding grounds for disease. Patients lay on filthy, blood-soaked floors with festering wounds. Infections spread rampantly. The stench of sickness and death filled the air. Even basic hygiene like handwashing was neglected. These appalling conditions greeted Nightingale at the Scutari Barracks Hospital during the Crimean War.

Nightingale understood sanitation, nutrition, and compassionate care were essential for effective healthcare. Where others saw no link between cleanliness and health, she made hygiene central. She insisted on regular cleaning, fresh bedding, and open windows for air flow. She established a laundry for clean linens. Though seemingly simple, these practices were revolutionary.

Similarly, Nightingale emphasized nutrition's vital role, unlike typical hospital fare. She ensured patients received fresh, nutritious meals and special diets for the gravely ill. Again, her emphasis on food's role in healing departed from the norm.

Most remarkably, Nightingale centered her approach on compassion - the idea that emotional support aided healing. This contrasted the era's view of patients as mere disease vessels. She and her nurses spent countless bedside hours listening, writing letters, and offering comfort. Treating patients with dignity was radically different.

Results spoke volumes.

But Nightingale's impact extended far beyond Crimea. Her vision of nursing as a respected, science-based profession was transformative. Establishing the first secular nursing school codified and carried her principles forward. This rippled outward, elevating possibilities for women's healthcare roles and society broadly.

Many Nightingale practices like handwashing, record-keeping, and statistics remain healthcare cornerstones today. Her emphasis on evidence-based approaches contrasted medicine's often haphazard methods then. She was a visionary anticipating 21st century tenets.

Yet her greatest legacy may be an unwavering belief in every patient's dignity and worth. When rigid hierarchies prevailed and the poor were expendable, she insisted on the highest standard for all. Her commitment to this - that every life merits compassion - remains urgently relevant.

As we navigate modern healthcare, Nightingale inspires us to combine scientific excellence with deep humanity. While medicine evolves rapidly, the core values she embodied - care, compassion, evidence, and patient advocacy - remain bedrock for nursing and healthcare broadly. In this era of sophisticated diagnostics and treatments, these fundamentally human qualities define healthcare's best.

Who Dared to Care?

Dark and dismal 19th-century hospitals were breeding grounds for disease and death. Who dared care for the sick and suffering under such dire conditions? At a time when nursing was seen as lowly work fit only for society's outcasts, one remarkable woman challenged this view and revolutionized healthcare - Florence Nightingale, the Lady with the Lamp.

Why does Nightingale's story still matter today? We often take skilled, compassionate nursing care for granted, forgetting the grim realities of the past. Imagine being ill or injured in the 1800s. You would lie in a filthy, overcrowded ward amid moans and stench. Nurses, if you could call them that, were often drunk, abusive, or utterly untrained - more likely to rob you than provide care. This bleak reality sparked Nightingale's calling.

Multiple issues plagued healthcare then. Nursing lacked respect as a skilled profession. Hospitals fostered infections due to poor hygiene. Doctors dismissed nurses as mere servants, not healthcare partners. Patients suffered needlessly; many died from preventable causes. People accepted sickness and death as God's will, seeing no hope for change. Nurses merely emptied bedpans and removed corpses, lacking real training or expertise.

Nightingale refused to accept this dire status quo. She envisioned nursing as a life-saving, noble vocation and made it reality. Her revolutionary yet simple approach: rigorously train nurses in health, hygiene, and patient care. Insist on cleanliness to curb illness transmission. Promote fresh air, nutrition, and healing environments. Tirelessly raise nursing's respectability as a profession.

Chapter 2: Principles of the Pioneering Nurse

To truly appreciate Florence Nightingale's immense impact, we must understand the true meanings behind phrases like "sanitation revolution," "nursing," and "compassionate care." These terms capture the profound shift in healthcare that Nightingale pioneered. By exploring their essence, we lay the groundwork to understand how one woman's relentless dedication transformed medicine forever.

The "sanitation revolution" seems clinical and sterile, yet it holds the key to countless lives saved. In Nightingale's era, cleanliness in hospitals was far from normal. These facilities were notoriously filthy, with disease rampant and hygiene an afterthought. It took a visionary like Nightingale to recognize that cleanliness wasn't merely aesthetic - it was a matter of life and death.

Imagine the stench of a 19th-century hospital ward - the acrid smell of festering wounds, the suffocating odor of unwashed bodies, the cloying scent of disease and decay. This was the battleground where Nightingale waged her war against infection. With fierce determination and belief in cleanliness, she transformed these dens of despair into sanctuaries of healing.

Nightingale's sanitation revolution wasn't a single sweeping change, but a series of small, deliberate actions. She insisted on regular handwashing, fresh linens, and proper ventilation. She understood that invisible germs were the true enemy, and she fought them with soap, water, sunlight, and fresh air.

Through tireless efforts, Nightingale proved sanitation wasn't a luxury but a necessity. By keeping hospitals clean, she showed lives could be saved and suffering alleviated. Her sanitation revolution laid the foundation for modern infection control practices.

Nightingale saw nursing differently - as a noble calling requiring skill, knowledge, and compassion. She believed properly trained nurses could be vital partners in healing, working alongside doctors. To bring this vision to life, she established the first professional nursing school at St. Thomas' Hospital in London.

At her school, Nightingale laid the groundwork for modern nursing education with a rigorous curriculum emphasizing practical skills, character, discipline, and empathy. She understood nursing wasn't just tasks like giving medicine - it was about seeing patients as whole people with physical, emotional, and spiritual needs.

Through her school and writings, Nightingale redefined nursing as a respectable, essential profession. She elevated nurses from servants to skilled caregivers with vital roles in healthcare. Her legacy lives on through the countless nurses following her path of dedication.

The concept of "compassionate care" may best capture Nightingale's essence. At a time when patients were seen as mere vessels of disease, she recognized the inherent dignity and humanity in every individual. True healing required emotional and spiritual support, not just physical intervention.

To Nightingale, compassionate care meant treating each patient with kindness, respect, and empathy. It meant listening to their concerns, alleviating fears, and offering hope. It meant seeing beyond illness to the person, recognizing every life is precious and deserves care.

This philosophy of compassion was revolutionary then, yet remains vital today. In a healthcare system that feels cold and impersonal, Nightingale's legacy reminds us of human connection's importance. It reminds us that behind every chart is a unique person with their own story, struggles, and healing hopes.

Florence Nightingale's groundbreaking approach revolutionized nursing and healthcare reform. Her core principles defined her work and legacy, inspiring healthcare professionals to this day. Let's explore these pioneering principles:

1. Evidence-based practice: Nightingale firmly believed in using evidence to drive change. She meticulously collected and analyzed data on mortality rates, hospital conditions, and

patient care. This data identified problems and guided effective solutions. During the Crimean War, her evidence-based reforms at the Barrack Hospital reduced the mortality rate from 42% to just 2%. Her famous "Rose Diagram" visually represented preventable deaths due to poor sanitation, compelling authorities to act.

2. Holistic patient care: Nightingale treated the whole person, not just physical ailments. She recognized that health is influenced by physical, psychological, social, and environmental factors. Nightingale emphasized creating a healing environment with fresh air, natural light, clean water, and nutritious food. She also provided compassionate emotional support, recognizing its role in recovery. Nightingale advocated respecting patients' religious and cultural beliefs, promoting humane treatment for all.

3. Hygiene and sanitation: Nightingale's emphasis on hygiene and sanitation was revolutionary. She recognized unsanitary conditions contributed to high mortality rates.

During the Crimean War, she transformed the filthy Barrack Hospital by scrubbing surfaces, providing clean linens and better food. Nightingale tirelessly advocated for sanitary reforms, using data to prove cleanliness was essential for patient care.

4. Advocacy for healthcare reform: Nightingale advocated for systemic reforms to improve healthcare access and quality. Her meticulous reports, like the 830-page document for the Royal Commission, exposed preventable deaths and pushed for change. She campaigned to improve military and civilian hospitals, influencing hospital design, sanitation, and patient comfort. Nightingale also pushed for better nursing education, establishing the Nightingale Training School.

5. Continuous learning and education: Nightingale was a lifelong learner, constantly expanding her knowledge to improve nursing practice. Her broad education allowed her to approach problems from multiple perspectives. She believed nurses needed strong theoretical knowledge and practical skills. The Nightingale Training School

combined classroom instruction with hospital experience. Nightingale advocated for nursing schools worldwide, shaping curricula to include public health and social welfare.

Nightingale's principles revolutionized nursing and healthcare, shaping modern practices. Her evidence-based, holistic, and compassionate approach elevated patient care standards. Her advocacy promoted lasting reforms, improving access and quality. Nightingale's commitment to continuous learning ensured nursing remained a dynamic, evolving profession. Today, nurses honor her legacy by upholding these principles, advancing healthcare for all.

Chapter 3: Understanding Florence

A wealthy woman of privilege abandoned high society to revolutionize healthcare forever. This was Florence Nightingale's remarkable life journey. Born into an aristocratic Victorian English family, she seemed destined for a life of luxury and leisure. But Nightingale defied societal expectations and chose a revolutionary path transforming nursing and healthcare reform.

In the 19th century, women of Nightingale's class were expected to marry well, manage households, and pursue feminine hobbies like needlework. The idea of a lady working, especially in nursing's gritty and gruesome field, was scandalous. Hospitals were filthy places where the poor went to die, not heal. In this context, Nightingale's choice to pursue nursing was downright rebellious.

What compelled her? A combination of deep faith, keen intellect, and unwavering purpose drove Nightingale. From youth, she felt a divine calling to serve others, believing God planned this for her life. This spiritual sense of mission paired with a brilliant, inquiring scientific mind. Despite her family's vehement opposition, Nightingale was resolute: "Now, Lord, let me think only of Thy will."

This iron-clad purpose propelled Nightingale through immense obstacles. In the Crimean War's Barrack Hospital, she encountered scenes of unspeakable horror amid filth, disease, and death. But she persisted, instituting rigorous sanitation, nutrition, and compassionate care protocols.

Beyond this hospital, Nightingale leveraged her newfound fame to advocate for healthcare policy changes. She lobbied for sanitary reforms, nurse education, and used statistics proving hygiene's life-saving impact. Though facing skepticism, she persevered, letting tangible patient outcome improvements sway critics.

Nightingale's journey teaches listening to our inner voice even when defying norms. It shows data and evidence's power to drive change. Ultimately, her legacy testifies to compassion's force coupled with determination. In today's healthcare challenges, her principles of questioning norms, leveraging data, and leading with compassion remain vital.

Breaking Barriers: Understanding Florence's World

To fully appreciate Florence Nightingale's revolutionary journey, we need to first understand the world she challenged. Her story showcases not just personal triumph but the power of breaking barriers amid Victorian societal norms, gender roles, and antiquated medical practices.

Victorian societal norms were rigid expectations dictating every aspect of life - dress, behavior, one's very purpose. But beneath the surface, these seemingly immutable rules masked a society grappling with rapid change. The old ways began cracking under progress's weight. Florence was born into this world, where women were expected to conform to narrow roles, and the idea of a woman working outside the home scandalous.

Gender roles in the 19th century differed vastly from today's relative equality. Society viewed women as delicate creatures suited only for the domestic sphere - managing households, raising children, pursuing genteel hobbies like needlework and painting. Pursuing a career, especially a field as gritty as nursing, was unthinkable for women. Men, conversely, were breadwinners, decision-makers shaping the world outside the home. This rigid division reflected deeply held beliefs about inherent differences between genders.

Nursing in Florence's time bore little resemblance to today's highly trained, respected profession. Hospitals were dirty, disease-ridden places where the poor went to die, not heal. Nurses were often unskilled laborers performing menial tasks like cleaning bedpans and changing linens, with little regard for their safety. Florence stepped into this grim reality, armed with unwavering purpose and determination to drive change.

19th-century medical practices reflected limited disease and human body understanding. Doctors relied heavily on bloodletting, purging, and other harmful practices often causing more harm than good. Sanitation was virtually nonexistent, with surgeons operating in dirty conditions and reusing instruments without cleaning. The germ theory of disease was novel, and many doctors scoffed at handwashing or basic hygiene. In this context, Florence's emphasis on cleanliness, fresh air, and proper nutrition was revolutionary.

The Spark of Rebellion

In Victorian England's rigid society, young Florence Nightingale yearned to forge her own path. She was a woman searching for purpose beyond the narrow confines of domestic life. Florence's early encounters with suffering sparked a fire within her - one that would ultimately transform healthcare.

Born into an affluent British family, Florence enjoyed a privileged upbringing filled with fine education and social connections. Yet even as a child, she sensed a deeper calling beyond domesticity. Her inquisitive mind drew her to the sciences, while her compassionate heart ached for the less fortunate.

As a teenager, Florence glimpsed the harsh realities hidden beneath Victorian society's polished veneer. On a family trip through the countryside, she witnessed scenes of abject poverty and illness that would haunt her forever. In squalid hovels and desperate eyes, she saw not just individual tragedies but a systemic failure demanding change.

Moved by these encounters, Florence sought opportunities to aid the sick and destitute wherever she went. She visited local hospitals and poorhouses, offering untrained but caring hands. Each experience fueled her conviction that she was destined for more than society's prescribed roles.

Florence's biggest struggle was reconciling her ambitions with her family's expectations. Like others of their class, her parents considered nursing unfit for a woman of her standing. They urged domestic tranquility, insisting her desire was a passing fancy.

But Florence knew this was no whimsy – it was a spiritual calling that superseded all obligations. In private, she spoke of experiencing a divine summons to alleviate suffering. Emboldened by this higher purpose, she defied limitations, turned down suitors, and sought every chance to expand her medical knowledge.

These formative experiences crystallized Florence's resolve to shatter barriers. If society deemed nursing unacceptable, she would change society itself. If women were seen as unfit for tending the sick, she would prove them indispensable.

Her pivotal moment came in 1853 when she became superintendent at London's Institution for Sick Gentlewomen. Florence implemented revolutionary reforms putting patient welfare first. She trained nurses, improved sanitation, and gathered data to guide decisions. The improved outcomes proved what she always knew: compassion, cleanliness and science could transform healthcare.

When the Crimean War erupted in 1854, Florence seized an unprecedented opportunity. Britain's Secretary of War asked her to assemble nurses for military hospitals.

Shocking society, she accepted without hesitation.

As Florence set sail with 38 nurses, she embarked not just on a mission but a war against disease, suffering, and society's limits on women. She could not foresee the trials and triumphs ahead – ones that would forever alter modern nursing.

Reflecting on Florence's early life, we see a woman unafraid to defy norms in pursuit of her calling. Her story reminds us that real change often sparks from a single act of rebellion – the courage to envision a better way. By following her convictions, Florence lit a path for generations of healers.

As later chapters reveal, the Crimean War put Florence's ideas to the ultimate test. Against unimaginable odds, she demonstrated the life-saving impact of sanitation, nutrition and compassionate care. In doing so, she transformed nursing and society's view of women's capabilities in healthcare.

Yet Florence's greatest legacy may be the enduring lesson of her early life: that an unshakable sense of purpose, fueled by grit, can topple even the most entrenched barriers. In rebelling against a world intent on limiting her, Florence Nightingale became an unstoppable force of change – one whose impact still echoes throughout modern medicine.

Conclusion

In a cold, hard Victorian society, what drove Florence Nightingale to spend her life in service? What we find when we look at her story was a profound sense of duty and an unwavering commitment to compassion and care for the suffering. To turn her back on a life of wealth and privilege took amazing bravery and courage.

Despite facing substantial opposition from her family and societal norms that viewed nursing as an unsuitable profession for a woman of her standing, Nightingale pursued her vocation with relentless determination. She sought knowledge across Europe, learning from various medical practices and embracing the principles of hygiene and patient care that were often neglected.

Her experience during the Crimean War, where she witnessed the appalling conditions of military hospitals, solidified her resolve. Nightingale's firsthand encounters with the suffering and neglect of soldiers propelled her to implement groundbreaking reforms in sanitation and medical care. Her tireless work during this period not only saved countless lives but also laid the foundation for modern nursing practices.

Florence Nightingale's drive was rooted in a profound empathy and a visionary approach to healthcare. She saw beyond the immediate needs, understanding that systemic change was essential for lasting impact.

Her legacy of compassion, evidence-based practice, and dedication to public health reforms continued to influence the field of nursing and healthcare long after her passing, embodying her lifelong commitment to service in a society that often overlooked the vulnerable and suffering.